A Pacific Northwest Publisher

Enigma | Michael Rigney

Enigma

Dedicated to Luke

By
Michael Rigney

Printed and bound in the United States of America.

First printing, 2012

ISBN-10: 0982858760
ISBN-13: 978-0-9828587-6-9

Published by Broken Publications

Broken Publications
PO Box 685
Eatonville, WA 98328

www.BrokenPublications.com

Edited by Jennifer-Crystal Johnson
Book cover by Jennifer-Crystal Johnson
www.JenniferCrystalJohnson.com

For more about Michael David Rigney, visit:
www.DigitalOutsider.com

Enigma | Michael Rigney

Enigma | Michael Rigney

Enigma

e·nig·ma/iˈnigmə/

Noun: A person or thing that is mysterious, puzzling, or
difficult to understand.
A riddle or paradox.

Enigma | Michael Rigney

The boy who sat at the road side
had a two-string guitar

To play a dear song
where his mother had died
and fill up the hopes of her dreams

One string sang with sorrow
when it was plucked

It rung with great pain,
the digging, deepening song
of the boy's two-sided brain

The other string was finer
and more costly
but it sang with a joy
oh so bright

Yes, the second string was lovely
and it cured the cold of night

So the boy who sat at the road side
with his two-sided brain
and with only two strings
to play for his fame

Made many songs sweet
and many songs sharp

They cured where they cut

A powerful harp

The agony and the ecstasy

The tired hand
Shivering

The bodies
without markers

It is filled with
beautiful,
intermittent
blips of light

The dream
keeps him awake

She said

Handing to him
the bones of creation

"They are for you."

She said

Showing to him
the dream of his life

Ensuring him that
it would come true

"You are beautiful to me."

Enigma | Michael Rigney

Boy that is shining under the sun
with flowery eyes full of love

Finding peace in the satin
of fields, summer bright

Chasing off demons
that come in the night

His world
is just shaking

His eyes
flowing blue

With sky-colored dreams
as he hands them to you

From the red-purple-scarlet
of the lovingly starlit

Nights of the sober sun seeking
for all of the love he is speaking

To spread out his dreams under you
giving fragrance of incense
and candle light beams

While he, under the sun,
sits and dreams

That beautiful boy
sitting up in his tree
laughing and joking and staring at me
his song so sweet
I can see it there, smiling
and all of his chambers are tear-filled from crying

but wondrous clouds drifting by
will grow cold and blue-hued
as long as the angels still fly
when he passes himself to eternal reward
and files his paintings in cabinet drawers

but the sea was still writhing in pain
as the angels call out to save him, in vain

he climbs even higher as floods fill the ground
and playing his music for loving the sound
watery tears in rose-covered eyes
and beautiful truth found in beautiful lies

soul spent on swimming through troubled seas
still cover his vision with roses disease
and the angels still calling his name
to save him again from the window pane
but outside he sees all the lovely
that come cold and coursing above me

that beautiful boy
sitting up in his tree
laughing and joking and staring at me
his song so sweet
I can see it there, smiling
and all of his chambers are tear-filled from crying

It was eight million times over the sun
or at least we guessed that age
when we were about ten

four of us went up that hill
to count berries on a vine
making sure the sun had set
over eight million times

and it was ten days after
me and her, sitting kind
just rang a tune on an old brass
cling
and I popped my drum

bang bang

and it was eight million times
we sat back with wines
drank heavy, hits us
cigar smoke and vibrant youths

Enigma | Michael Rigney

The sun was still setting
over a thousand beliefs
and I'd breathe through my chest into you

then the spark of my letting her
cold comfort lives

I begged my beliefs
gave sacred relief
how the sweet summer curls
and it tore out a painting's blue hue

poverty stricken
they want to survive
but they bore all our children
from under my dresser
and gave all their daughters as wives

but the song and I'm swelling
a far richer fare
and I'm telling my secrets to you

how a sweet summer thrives
and the secret I'm speaking
they gave all their daughters as wives

Enigma | Michael Rigney

The darkness of night
and the furious storm
through the eye we will rest
and toil no more

but the passing away
of the blues of the morn
can linger no longer
as again we are torn

we know in the calm
That, once again
it will tear through our houses
through day we pretend

that in the calm winter
or summer or fall
the storm won't avail
and our homes will not fall

yet each time they fail
at the end of the eye
and the throngs of our people
carry burdens
they cry

to pray at our gods
why curse us as this?
what are our sins
that deny you our bliss?

but the just and the faithful
say sinner am I
so punish and teach me
but give peace whilst the eye

Enigma | Michael Rigney

It is an endless sea of souls
in which I am lost
as the beast slowly searches
for the ringing of the damned

and the angel from high
victory comes
to drag man from his pit
among the wicked and blind

yet he turns his eyes
'tis but a fairy tale
and all that I am
refuses to believe

for these dreams of the gods
and the balancing spirits
who guide him to waking
cloud his clouded eyes

to see clearly
is to be blind
and to be mad
is to see clearly
ignorance is the right of the damned

he who thinks he knows
does not yet understand

A coded secret of the moon
vibratory translation
another estimation
of universal harmony

figuring principalities
in the echo
it was washed away
and they discovered grace

the first set of chords
to a song lyric
an expression of certainty
in matters of dirt

an octave
a chord
ghostly order
universal agreement

music of the spheres
that's where it began

Born from the realm
yet unnamed
seeing itself becoming
in a place without position

The great father
Ahway
and his betrothed
Oeye

Born from one
which was
and was not
made two

Now three await
a birth within
it becomes

Joining together
in vast formation
burst forth seven

The children
were the night
and waking

Made of it
by names
which
Are

Ephemera

Ageless echoes
of ebbing tides
breaking waters on my back
as sinners throw their stones
killing another dream
before its time

wake with joy
after walking next to death
one more time
the wire never gets thicker
but the walker gets braver

dead heroes lead to death
trade my life for a perfect illustration
the thunder clap
is just a murmur to the crowd

the spirit beads my necklace
cutting away the string
but adding better beads
I take what should be earned
by stealing the ghosts' vibrations

the price is high to heavy hearts
but scentless to those who can't smell
my flesh falls to my knees
forgive my breaking bones

Cool jewel moon
on sun-kissed summer night
the calm before the storm
the time before the fight

two lovers tangle
as the vine
growing together, dancing
intoxicated by new wine
they hold the world aloft
to prevent the fall

warriors gather
two brutal factions
one at either end
the killing field awaits the call

trapped between them
the calm of the moon
the lovers' circle
and beams of life
which must go on
Eternal

the call is sounded
the warriors clash
to decide the battle
who wins at last

good or evil
dark or light
torment of the lost
or joy of pure delight

yet the lovers mingle
and notice not
what falls around them
as men are lost

and so enthralled
within each other's arms
the fight goes on
but they remain
unharmed

Enigma | Michael Rigney

Come upon
my
Moon

A darkness brings cool Summer Blue

I rest despite my feverish lust

Burning hearts flourish
in the misty passage

Between
fire and rain

Between
hope and desperation

My sorrow
cannot quench
the savage heart

Enigma | Michael Rigney

She reigns
As shadows in the night

Over the age of the moon
And terror

She rides
A wild stallion

Drinks from the Darkest cup

And runs her fingers
Through my hair

She murmurs peace for the willing
but keeps the slaves captive

A dream
Never so easily
Was forgotten

The stars open

A path
in the echo

Uniform
deformations
Contract

Her pearl eyes
Moist

I see beyond
the curtain

Rock musician
endless haze

Spring and summer
last for days

Deadbeat boyfriend
angel wings

Downy soft
pretty things

Tends to over-burden

Strings
the strung

Waving our ambitions
we become

Flurry

Let eternity rest
in a bed of its own

At least calmly
for one thousand years

We shall dance
with our lovers

And
Our star-covered others

Who, living much longer
knew all of our brothers

And
knowing them

Now they tell
stories

Enigma | Michael Rigney

Our old parted hearts

still singing in verse
A chord you had learned
long ago

A measure of time
With her beating heart Baking
In the sun
As you gave her the making

Now free from a burden
of rose-colored seas
Built from the blood
of a child's disease

Her terrified heart
once torn into ribbons
By grace of undoing
is free

And granted a Dream In return
He did love in the heart
as he learned

With peaceful dreams parted
Now walk in the sky
The love of a child
Can grow old and die

Fin